GIANT
GOODIES

SUPERSIZE YOUR SNACKS!

LOVE FOOD™

CONTENTS

Introduction 4

Giant Frosted Cupcake 8

Double-Dunk Choc-Chunk Cookie 11

Party-Size Popcorn Ball 14

Colossal Cake Pops 17

Foot-High Festive Cookie 21

Ginormous Gingerbread Man 25

Mighty Macaron 29

Humongous Heart Cookie 32

Plentiful Peanut Butter Cup 35

Bountiful Cinnamon Roll 39

Whopping Whoopie Pie 42

Awesome Apple Turnover 45

Massive Monster Cupcake 49

Pancake Peak 52

Mega Muffin 55

Chunky Chocolate Donut 59

Share-Size Sundae 62

Mammoth Mint Cream 65

Chock-a-Block Cookie Sandwich 69

Tremendous Truffles 72

Super Sweet & Salted Pretzels 75

Index 78

GO LARGE!

It's the foodie trend that's swept the Internet over the last few years—supersize snacks! From cakes, cookies, and other baked goods to chocolate bars and candies, you can make just about anything bigger and better than the original. *Giant Goodies* is a delicious selection of sweet treats that look amazing and taste just as good as their smaller counterparts.

So, just how large can you go? Well, there are obvious limitations to how big some of the goodies can be made. Cakes, pastries, and cookies have to fit in a domestic oven (unless you bake them in sections), whereas some goodies, such as the macaron, will be too fragile to lift if they are made any larger than the recipe states. Of course, practicality should always rule in the kitchen, so look out for hints and tips.

Once you've tried a few of the mega marvels in this book, you may be tempted to try upgrading some of your other favorites—and why not? We say if you like it, make it big enough to share!

BEFORE YOU START

There are a few things to check before you begin to create your giant goodies.

● Be sure that you have all the necessary ingredients, and in large enough quantities, to make your chosen recipe. Do not underestimate just how much chocolate is needed to make a giant chocolate truffle, or how many cups of milk go into a mile-high stack of pancakes—in *Giant Goodies*, we've supersized the lot!

● Clear a large enough space in your kitchen to work in—rolling out volumes of cookie dough or pie dough needs a pretty big area of worktop. Also, read through the recipe before starting, and, if necessary, make sure you have enough room for your giant goodie in the refrigerator or freezer.

● Check that you have big enough equipment for the task on hand—and if you don't, improvise! Mixing bowls should be as large as possible – mixing a large quantity of cake batter or cookie dough is a seriously messy business in a small bowl. Alternatively, you could use a dish-washing bowl (thoroughly washed and dried before use) to hold your giant creation. Large spatulas are also an essential piece of equipment—they help when transferring warm baked goods to a cooling rack with minimum drama. Baking pans and sheets will, of course, also need to be pretty big, but you'll need to check that they will fit in your oven before getting started!

● Invest in the very best ingredients you can afford—you'll see the benefit in both taste and texture, particularly with chocolate.

IMPROVISE!

If you've been paying attention, you'll know that most of the recipes in this book can be made with the everyday equipment that you have in your kitchen (given a little imagination). For best results, some, such as the giant cupcake, do require special cake molds, and where baking gadgets have been used you'll find them listed with the recipe—look out for the extra equipment notes. Decorative baking molds are readily available online, or find them in specialty kitchen shops and large department stores—they're a worthwhile purchase if you're going to commit to the *Giant Goodies* challenge, and you could always share the cost with a couple of baking buddies.

If you're baking on a budget, and don't want to splash out, we do have some alternative suggestions for great results.

- Cupcake—use a deep ovenproof baking dish or brioche pan with a 1-quart capacity for the bottom of the cake and a 5-inch round deep cake pan for the top of the cake. Grease and line the bottom of both the dish and the pan before adding the cake batter, and keep an eye on the baking time to be sure of a perfect cake. Once cooled, cut and trim the top cake to a domed shape using a serrated knife.

- Muffin—use a 1¼-quart ovenproof baking dish or brioche pan lined with the folded parchment paper.

- Donut—use two Bundt cake pans, each with a 3-cup capacity. Grease thoroughly before pouring in the cake batter and bake as per the existing instructions. Alternatively, divide the batter between two 8-inch round cake pans. Once baked and cooled, use a round cookie cutter to stamp out a hole from the center of each cake before sandwiching them together with the chocolate frosting.

A NOTE ABOUT COOKING TIMES

Because these recipes are supersize, cooking times and temperatures may seem completely different from a normal recipe. Ovens can vary considerably, depending on whether they are gas, electric, or convection, so it's best to use the oven temperature in the recipe as a guide and keep an eye on your giant goodies as they cook. If you know from previous baking experience that your oven runs a little hot or cold, then adjust the temperature accordingly. Convection ovens cook more quickly than conventional ovens so you need to reduce the temperature by about 25°F to compensate (or follow the manufacturers' guide). With a little common sense, you'll be baking big treats in no time!

BASIC BUTTERCREAM

To make the quantity necessary for the vanilla buttercream for the Giant Frosted Cupcake on page 8 and Massive Monster Cupcake on page 49, place 1¾ sticks of unsalted butter in a large bowl and beat with a handheld electric mixer until pale. Gradually beat in 3¼ cups confectioners' sugar and 1 teaspoon of vanilla extract, beating until pale and creamy. This frosting can then be piped, or spread, as desired!

Giant Frosted Cupcake

Light fluffy sponge, covered in a great big swirl of vanilla frosting—delicious!

SERVES: 12–14   PREP TIME: 50 mins   COOK TIME: 1 hour 20 mins–1 hour 30 mins

INGREDIENTS

3¼ cups all-purpose flour,
plus extra for dusting

1½ teaspoons baking powder

3 sticks butter, softened,
plus extra for greasing

1¾ cups granulated sugar

6 extra-large eggs

2 tablespoons milk

TO ASSEMBLE & DECORATE

2 tablespoons apricot preserves, warmed
and strained

1 pound pink ready-to-use fondant

confectioners' sugar, for dusting

1 quantity Basic Buttercream (see page 5)

1 candied cherry

pink and red candy-coated chocolate beans

1 Preheat the oven to 325°F. Thoroughly grease the cupcake mold with butter then dust lightly with flour, tipping out any excess. Place on a baking sheet and set aside.

2 Sift the flour and the baking powder into a large bowl and add the remaining ingredients. Using a handheld electric mixer, beat until the mixture is pale and creamy. Divide the batter between the prepared molds, making a slight dip in the center of each.

3 Bake in the preheated oven for 1 hour 20 minutes, or until risen, golden, and a toothpick inserted into each cake comes out clean. Remove the top cake from the oven, and bake the bottom cake for another 10 minutes. Remove the bottom cake from the oven. Let both cakes cool in the molds for 10–15 minutes, then carefully turn out onto a cooling rack and let cool completely.

4 Trim the top of each cake to create a level surface. Place the bottom cake upside down on a board and brush all over with the preserves. Roll out the fondant on a surface dusted with confectioners' sugar to an 11-inch circle. Drape the fondant over the bottom cake, smoothing the sides. Carefully lift the cake and place it upright on a cake board or flat plate. Fold the edges of the fondant over the top of the cake, trimming off any excess.

5 Spread a layer of buttercream over the top of the bottom cake, then spoon the rest into a large pastry bag.

6 Position the top cake firmly on the bottom cake. Pipe the buttercream all over the top cake—work in one continuous swirl from the bottom to the top, then smooth. Decorate with a candied cherry and candy-coated chocolate beans.

1

3

6

You will also need ...

A giant cupcake mold, with a 5-cup capacity bottom and a 3½-cup top.

Double-Dunk Choc-Chunk Cookie

What could be better than a chewy, sticky, chocolatey cookie with a giant glass of milk? Two of them!

SERVES: 8 each   PREP TIME: 25 mins   COOK TIME: 25–30 mins

INGREDIENTS

2 sticks butter, softened, plus extra for greasing

1 cup firmly packed light brown sugar

2 tablespoons light corn syrup

2¾ cups all-purpose flour

2¾ teaspoons baking powder

6 ounces milk chocolate, chopped into chunks

1 Preheat the oven to 350°F. Grease two large baking sheets and set aside.

2 Put the butter and sugar into a bowl and beat together until pale and creamy, then beat in the corn syrup. Sift in half the flour with the baking powder and mix in, then sift in the remaining flour and add the chocolate. Stir until the mixture starts to clump together, then gather it together with your hands and lightly knead to form a soft dough.

3 Divide the dough in half. Shape each piece into a ball and place one ball on each prepared baking sheet. Press out each ball with your hands to a flat circle with a diameter of about 8 inches. Make the edges of each circle a little thicker than the center to allow for spreading.

Not a chocoholic?

Swap the milk chocolate for 1 cup of macadamia nuts or try ½ cup of pecans mixed with ½ cup raisins instead.

4 Bake one cookie in the preheated oven for 15 minutes. Remove the baking sheet from the oven and, using a spatula, reshape the edges of the cookie to form a neat 11-inch, round cookie. Reduce the oven temperature to 325°F. Return the cookie to the oven and bake for an additional 8–12 minutes, until golden brown. Increase the oven temperature to 350°F and bake the second cookie in the same way.

5 Let the cookies cool on the baking sheets for at least 25 minutes. Slide a large spatula under each cookie to loosen it from the baking sheet, then carefully transfer to a wire rack to cool completely.

Hints & tips

For round, perfectly formed cookies use an 8-inch cake pan to shape before baking.

Party-Size Popcorn Ball

Airy popcorn and crisp caramel combine to make a sweet snack fit for any movie marathon!

SERVES: 2–3   **PREP TIME:** 20 mins   **COOK TIME:** 15 mins

INGREDIENTS

1 tablespoon sunflower oil

½ cup popping corn

1 cup sugar

2 tablespoons light corn syrup

⅔ cup water

butter, for shaping

1 Line a baking sheet with parchment paper and set aside. Heat the oil in a large, deep saucepan with a lid. Add the corn, cover the pan, and cook over high heat, shaking the pan frequently, until all the corn has popped. Transfer to a large, heatproof bowl, discarding any unpopped or burned corn.

2 Put the sugar, syrup, and water into a large, heavy saucepan and heat gently, stirring continuously, until the sugar has dissolved. Increase the heat and boil the mixture for 5–6 minutes, without stirring, until a golden caramel has formed.

3 Quickly pour the caramel over the popcorn and mix well. When the popcorn is just cool enough to handle, use buttered hands to shape into a large ball. Place on the prepared baking sheet and let cool.

Colossal Cake Pops

These sweet cake-based treats might look pretty in pink, but they pack a mean flavor punch!

SERVES: 4–6 each   **PREP TIME:** 30 mins (plus chilling)   **COOK TIME:** 5–10 mins

INGREDIENTS

1½ sticks unsalted butter, softened

1¾ cups confectioners' sugar, sifted

1 (1 pound) lemon-flavor pound cake

7 ounces pink candy melts

sugar sprinkles and pink edible cake-decorating glitter, to decorate

YOU WILL ALSO NEED

3 (8-inch) cake pop sticks

3 tall glasses filled with pie weights or dried beans

1 Line a plate with parchment paper and set aside. Put the butter into a bowl and gradually beat in the confectioners' sugar to make a smooth buttercream.

2 Finely crumble the pound cake with your fingertips or in a food processor and add to the buttercream. Mix thoroughly with a wooden spoon. Divide the mixture into three pieces and shape each piece into a ball by rolling between the palms of your hands. Don't roll too much at this stage or the buttercream will start to melt and make the mixture too sticky to handle.

3 Place the cake balls on the prepared plate and chill in the refrigerator for 2–3 hours, until solid. To achieve perfectly round, smooth shapes, remove the cake balls from the refrigerator 2–3 times during the first hour of chilling and reroll on a flat surface or board.

Top of the pops

For best results, use a moist cake base to make the cake balls. This can be any flavor you want—we've used lemon-flavor pound cake for a zesty kick.

4 To decorate, place the candy melts in a double boiler or a heatproof bowl set over a saucepan of barely simmering water and heat until melted. Remove from the heat and stir until smooth, then let cool for 5 minutes. Meanwhile, place the decorations into separate, shallow bowls. Once cooled, dip the end of each cake pop stick into the melted candy and then push into the center of the cake ball.

5 Dip each cake ball in the melted candy to coat. Use a spoon to spread the coating evenly over each cake ball, making sure there are no gaps. Hold over the bowl to let any excess coating drip back into the bowl, then lightly dip into the sprinkles before the coating starts to set.

6 Stand each decorated cake pop upright in a filled glass (the weights will stop the weight of the cake from tipping over the glass) and let stand in a cool place until the coating has set completely.

Foot-High Festive Cookie

Celebrate the season of excess with a ginormous festive treat—a perfect size for sharing.

SERVES: 14–16   PREP TIME: 1 hour 30 mins (plus chilling)   COOK TIME: 45–50 mins

INGREDIENTS

2½ sticks butter, softened,
plus extra for greasing

1½ cups granulated sugar

1 extra-large egg

1 extra-large egg yolk

5⅓ cups all-purpose flour

TO ASSEMBLE AND DECORATE

2 egg whites

4 cups confectioners' sugar,
plus extra for dusting

few drops lemon juice

green food coloring

4 ounces red ready-to-use fondant

gold edible cake-decorating glitter

colored candy-coated chocolate beans

1 Grease a large baking sheet and set aside. Put the butter and sugar into a large bowl and beat with a handheld electric mixer until pale and creamy. Beat in the egg and egg yolk. Sift in the flour and mix with a wooden spoon until the mixture starts to clump together. Using your hands, gently knead to a smooth, soft dough. Flatten into a thick circle and wrap in plastic wrap. Chill in the refrigerator for about 45 minutes, until firm.

2 Roll out the dough between two large sheets of plastic wrap to a thickness of ⅜ inch. Using the paper template as a guide, cut out a tree shape. Reroll the scraps and use to cut out a base for the tree, about 7 inches wide across the top and 3½ inches high. Use the cookie cutter to stamp out a small star. Place the tree and base on the baking sheet and put the star on a small plate.

You will also need ...

A Christmas tree paper template (about 15 inches high and 13 inches across the bottom) and a small star-shape cookie cutter.

21

6

8

6 Place the tree cookie on a large board and use some of the white icing to attach the base cookie to the tree, firmly pressing them together. Spread the green icing all over the upper part of the tree, swirling it with a small spatula.

7 Decorate the star with some of the reserved white icing, sprinkle with edible gold glitter, and attach it to the top of the tree with a little more icing.

8 Roll out the ready-to-use red fondant on a surface dusted with confectioners' sugar and use to cover the base cookie, attaching it with a little of the white icing. Spoon any remaining white icing into a pastry bag fitted with a small round tip. Pipe a scalloped border along the top of the red base—to cover the seam between the base and tree. Pipe a zigzag pattern across the green part of the tree and decorate with candy-coated chocolate beans. Let set.

3 Chill the cookie shapes in the refrigerator for 45 minutes. Meanwhile, preheat the oven to 350°F.

4 Bake the tree and base in the preheated oven for 20 minutes. Remove the base with a spatula and place on a wire rack to cool. Cover the tips of the tree with aluminum foil to prevent them from overbrowning and return to the oven. Bake for an additional 10–12 minutes, until pale golden. Let cool on the baking sheet for 10 minutes, then transfer to a wire rack to cool completely. Transfer the star to the baking sheet and bake for 10–12 minutes, until pale golden. Transfer to the wire rack to cool completely.

5 To assemble, place the egg whites and half the confectioners' sugar in a large bowl and beat with a handheld electric mixer until blended and smooth, then add the remaining confectioners' sugar and lemon juice and continue beating until smooth and thick. Reserve ⅓ cup of the icing, cover and set aside. Use the green food coloring to color the remaining icing, mixing until the shade is consistent.

Ginormous Gingerbread Man

It might seem like the stuff of fairy tales, but this is a supersize story-time treat!

SERVES: 15–20   PREP TIME: 1 hour (plus cooling)   COOK TIME: 25–30 mins

INGREDIENTS

7¼ cups all-purpose flour, plus extra for dusting

2 tablespoons ground ginger

2 teaspoons baking soda

2 sticks butter, plus extra for greasing

⅔ cup light corn syrup

1½ cups firmly packed light brown sugar

2 extra-large eggs, beaten

TO ASSEMBLE AND DECORATE

1 egg white, lightly beaten

2 cups confectioners' sugar, sifted, plus extra for dusting

few drops lemon juice

1 pound white ready-to-use fondant

red food coloring

1 Preheat the oven to 350°F. Grease two large baking sheets and set aside. Sift the flour, ginger, and baking soda into a bowl and make a well in the center.

2 Put the butter, corn syrup, and sugar into a large saucepan and heat gently, stirring continuously, until the butter has melted and the sugar has dissolved. Pour into the flour mixture, add the eggs, and mix to a firm dough. Gently knead until smooth.

3 Turn out the dough onto a large floured surface and roll out to a thickness of ⅝ inch. Place the paper template on the dough and use a sharp knife to cut out the gingerbread man.

You will also need ...

A gingerbread man paper template (about 16 inches wide and 20 inches high).

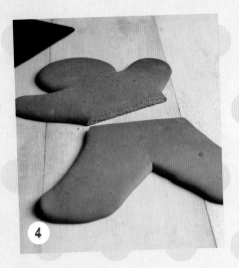

4

7

Fashion fix

Our gingerbread man is all set to run, run as fast as he can in a dashing pair of dungarees— dress yours however you see fit!

4 Cut the gingerbread man into two pieces across the middle of the body. Very carefully lift each piece onto the prepared baking sheets. Bake in the preheated oven for 25–30 minutes, until golden.

5 While the gingerbread halves are still hot, and still on the baking sheets, use a sharp knife to trim the straight edges— this will help you to make a smoother seam when assembling the gingerbread later. Slide a spatula under the hot gingerbread to loosen it from the baking sheets, then let cool on the baking sheets for 10 minutes.

Carefully transfer both pieces of gingerbread to a wire rack and let cool completely.

6 To assemble and decorate, first make the royal icing. Put the egg white and confectioners' sugar into a bowl and beat with a handheld electric mixer until smooth and thick, adding a few drops of lemon juice once combined. Place the gingerbread halves on a large board or tray and use some of the royal icing to join them together. Let set, and cover the remaining royal icing and set aside.

7 Reserve one-quarter of the white ready-to-use fondant and use the red food coloring to color the remainder. Roll out the red icing on a surface dusted with confectioners' sugar and cut out shorts and suspenders. Attach to the gingerbread man with more of the royal icing—the top edge of the shorts should cover the seam in the gingerbread. Shape the white fondant into buttons and attach with a little more of the royal icing.

8 Spoon any remaining royal icing into a pastry bag fitted with a small round tip and pipe wavy lines on the arms and legs and to add eyes and a mouth. Let set.

Mighty Macaron

It's not the dainty little morsel you might find in a French pâtisserie, but it tastes delicious!

SERVES: 12   PREP TIME: 40 mins   COOK TIME: 30–35 mins

INGREDIENTS

1½ cups ground almonds (almond meal)

1¾ cups confectioners' sugar, plus extra for dusting

4 extra-large egg whites

½ cup superfine sugar (or the same amount of granulated sugar processed in a food processor for 1 minute)

red food coloring

FILLING

2 cups cream

¼ cup raspberry preserves

1½ cups fresh raspberries

1 Put the ground almonds and confectioners' sugar into a food processor and process for 15 seconds. Sift the mixture into a bowl. Line two baking sheets with parchment paper, mark each with a 9-inch circle, and set aside.

2 Place the egg whites in a large bowl and whisk until they hold soft peaks. Gradually whisk in the superfine sugar to make a firm, glossy meringue. Using a spatula, fold the almond mixture into the meringue, one-third at a time. Fold the food coloring in with the last third of the meringue. When all the dry ingredients are thoroughly incorporated, continue to cut and fold the mixture until it forms a shiny batter with a thick ribbonlike consistency.

Baking day

A damp atmosphere will have an adverse affect on your macarons—save yourself a ruined batch and wait for a hot, dry day!

3 Divide the mixture between the prepared baking sheets, using a spatula to ease it out to the edge of each marked circle. Tap the baking sheets firmly on a surface to remove any air bubbles and level the surfaces. Let stand at room temperature for 30 minutes. Meanwhile, preheat the oven to 325°F.

4 Bake the macarons in the preheated oven for 30–35 minutes, until crisp on top. If you don't have a convection oven, swap the baking sheets around halfway through cooking (or bake one macaron at a time). Turn off the oven, keep the door slightly ajar, and let the meringues cool inside until completely cold.

5 To make the filling, whip the cream until it holds soft peaks. Carefully turn one macaron upside down on a flat serving plate and gently peel off the parchment paper. Spread with the preserves and top with the whipped cream. Arrange the raspberries on top of the cream, then carefully remove the parchment paper from the second macaron and gently place it on top of the filling.

Humongous Heart Cookie

There's a whole lot of love packed into this cute heart-shape cookie.

SERVES: 8   PREP TIME: 20 mins (plus chilling)   COOK TIME: 20–25 mins

INGREDIENTS

1 stick butter, softened, plus extra for greasing

⅓ cup granulated sugar

1 teaspoon vanilla extract

1 extra-large egg yolk

1⅔ cups all-purpose flour, plus extra for dusting

TO DECORATE

2 tablespoons beaten egg white

1⅓ cups confectioners' sugar, plus extra for dusting

few drops lemon juice

10 ounces pink ready-to-use fondant

YOU WILL ALSO NEED

heart-shape paper template (about 9 inches across the widest part)

1 Line a baking sheet with parchment paper and set aside. Put the butter and sugar into a bowl and beat together until pale and creamy. Beat in the vanilla extract and egg yolk. Sift in the flour and mix to a soft dough. Turn out onto a floured surface and lightly knead until smooth, adding more flour as necessary.

2 Flatten the dough to a 6-inch circle and place on the prepared sheet. Place the paper template on the dough and use a sharp knife to cut out the heart shape. Reserve the template. Chill the dough in the refrigerator for 30 minutes. Meanwhile, preheat the oven to 350°F.

3 Place the baking sheet in the preheated oven and bake for 20–25 minutes, until pale golden. Let cool on the sheet for 30 minutes, then transfer to a wire rack to cool completely.

4 To make the royal icing, place the egg white and confectioners' sugar in a bowl and beat with a handheld electric mixer until smooth and thick, adding a few drops of lemon juice, if needed. Thinly roll out the ready-to-use fondant on a surface dusted with confectioners' sugar and use the paper template as a guide to cut out a heart shape—cut the fondant about ⅔ inch smaller than the cookie on all sides. Spread a little royal icing over the cookie and secure the pink fondant heart to the surface.

5 Spoon the remaining royal icing into a pastry bag fitted with a small round tip and pipe a border around the edge of the fondant. Then work around the border, creating a scalloped edge. Let set overnight.

Plentiful Peanut Butter Cup

A whopping version of a confectionery classic, this chocolate cup has it all!

SERVES: 12   PREP TIME: 40 mins (plus chilling)   COOK TIME: 10 mins

INGREDIENTS

1 cup smooth peanut butter

½ cup firmly packed light brown sugar

1 teaspoon vanilla extract

6 tablespoons butter

1 cup confectioners' sugar

12 ounces milk chocolate, broken into pieces

12 ounces semisweet chocolate, broken into pieces

YOU WILL ALSO NEED

2 (8-inch) round nonstick cake liners

9-inch solid tart pan

1 To make the filling, put the peanut butter, brown sugar, vanilla extract, and half the butter into a saucepan and heat gently until the butter and sugar have dissolved, stirring continuously. Simmer for 2–3 minutes, then remove from the heat and gradually beat in the confectioners' sugar. Transfer to a bowl and let cool.

2 Put the milk chocolate, semisweet chocolate, and remaining butter into a large double boiler or a large heatproof bowl set over a saucepan of barely simmering water and heat until melted, stirring occasionally. Remove from the heat and stir until smooth.

Fancy fillings

Once you've made the bottom of the chocolate shell, you could fill this treat with almost anything—try marshmallow cream and raspberry preserves?

35

3 Place the cake liners in a double layer in the tart pan (this keeps the shape of the peanut butter cup and makes it easier to transfer to the refrigerator). Pour one-third of the chocolate mixture into the bottom of the liner. Transfer to the refrigerator and let stand for 20–30 minutes, until just set.

4 Shape the peanut butter mixture into a 7-inch circle and gently place it on top of the set chocolate.

5 If necessary, remelt the remaining chocolate in the double boiler or by placing the bowl over a saucepan of barely simmering water and stirring occasionally. Pour the remaining chocolate over the peanut butter filling to cover it completely, then gently level the surface. Chill in the refrigerator until set.

6 To serve, remove the peanut butter cup from the paper lining. Place on a flat serving plate and let stand at room temperature for about 1 hour, then slice into wedges with a sharp knife.

Bountiful Cinnamon Roll

Soft buttery dough with a cinnamon sugar filling and sweet icing make a bumper version of the classic pastry.

SERVES: 12   **PREP TIME:** 45 mins (plus proving)   **COOK TIME:** 20–25 mins

INGREDIENTS

3⅔ cups strong white bread flour, plus extra for dusting

¼ teaspoon salt

2¼ teaspoons (1 envelope) active dry yeast

3½ tablespoons granulated sugar

4 tablespoons butter, melted, plus extra for greasing

1 extra-large egg, beaten

1 cup warm milk

FILLING AND ICING

4 tablespoons butter, softened

¼ cup granulated sugar

¼ cup firmly packed dark brown sugar

2 teaspoons ground cinnamon

1⅔ cups confectioners' sugar

2–3 tablespoons warm water

1 Sift the flour and salt into a large bowl. Stir in the yeast and sugar and make a well in the center. Mix together the melted butter, egg, and milk in a small bowl and pour into the well. Mix to a soft, slightly sticky dough. Turn the dough onto a floured surface and knead for 5–6 minutes, until smooth and elastic, adding a little more flour if the dough is too sticky.

2 Place the dough in a bowl, cover with lightly oiled plastic wrap, and let stand in a warm place for 1 hour 15 minutes, or until doubled in size. Grease a 9-inch square cake pan.

Hints & tips

For a delicious alternative, sprinkle the roll with 1 cup of pecans before baking and add a few drops of vanilla extract to the icing.

Hints & tips

Overlap each new strip of dough with the previous strip by about 2 inches—this will make sure that the seams will stay sturdy when baked.

3 Turn the dough onto a floured surface and knead again lightly for 1 minute. Roll out to a 24 x 8-inch rectangle. Trim the edges with a pizza cutter or knife. Spread the softened butter over the dough. Mix together the granulated sugar, brown sugar, and cinnamon and spoon the mixture evenly over the butter, pressing down gently with the back of the spoon.

4 Use the pizza cutter to cut the dough into three long strips. Roll one of the strips up (from one short end) with the cinnamon butter on the inside of the roll, to create a swirl. Feed in a second dough strip by attaching the free edge of the rolled strip to one end of the new strip. Continue rolling to create a larger swirl. Repeat the process to add the final dough strip.

5 Turn the prepared cake pan over the dough swirl. Holding together the cake pan and board with your hands, flip them both over to transfer the dough swirl to the cake pan. Sprinkle any spilled cinnamon sugar around the dough swirl.

6 Cover loosely with lightly oiled plastic wrap and let stand in a warm place for 30–40 minutes, until the dough has risen and is just touching the sides of the pan. Meanwhile, preheat the oven to 400°F. Remove the plastic wrap and bake in the preheated oven for 20-25 minutes, until golden brown. Let cool in the pan for 15 minutes, then turn out onto a wire rack.

7 To make the icing, sift the confectioners' sugar into a large bowl and stir in enough of the warm water to make a smooth thick icing. Drizzle it over the warm roll, then let set.

Whopping Whoopie Pie

Dense, chocolatey sponge filled with a fluffy marshmallow cream—this is the ultimate treat.

SERVES: 8–10   **PREP TIME:** 45 mins (plus cooling and chilling)   **COOK TIME:** 25–30 mins

INGREDIENTS

1⅓ cups all-purpose flour

1½ teaspoons baking soda

½ cup unsweetened cocoa powder

6 tablespoons butter, softened,
plus extra for greasing

⅓ cup white vegetable shortening

¾ cup firmly packed dark brown sugar

1 extra-large egg, beaten

1 teaspoon vanilla extract

⅔ cup milk, plus 3 tablespoons for the filling

32 large white marshmallows
(about 8 ounces)

1¼ cups heavy cream

sprinkles, to decorate

YOU WILL ALSO NEED

2 (9-inch) round cake pans

1 Preheat the oven to 350°F. Grease the cake pans, line the bottoms with parchment paper, and set aside. Sift together the flour, baking soda, and cocoa powder into a bowl, stir to combine, and set aside.

2 Put the butter, vegetable shortening, and sugar into a large bowl and beat with a handheld electric mixer until pale and fluffy. Beat in the egg and vanilla extract, followed by half the flour mixture. Beat in the milk, then fold in the remaining flour mixture until thoroughly combined.

3 Divide the batter between the prepared pans, making a slight dome in the center of each. Bake in the preheated oven for 25–30 minutes, until risen and springy to the touch. Let the cakes cool in the pans for 10 minutes, then carefully turn out onto a wire rack to cool completely.

4 To make the filling, put the marshmallows and milk into a double boiler or a large heatproof bowl set over a saucepan of simmering water. Heat until the marshmallows have melted, stirring occasionally. Remove from the heat and let cool for 25 minutes.

5 Meanwhile, put the cream into a separate bowl and whip until it holds stiff peaks. Fold in the marshmallow mixture, then cover and chill in the refrigerator for 20–25 minutes, or until firm enough to spread.

6 Spread the marshmallow cream over one cake and top with the second cake, pressing it down gently. Roll the exposed sides of the marshmallow cream in sprinkles to decorate.

Awesome Apple Turnover

At three times the size of its common pastry cousins, this isn't a treat to be trifled with!

SERVES: 12–14   **PREP TIME:** 40 mins (plus cooling)   **COOK TIME:** 1 hour

INGREDIENTS

9 Granny Smith or other cooking apples (about 3 pounds), peeled, cored, and chopped

4 tablespoons butter, plus extra for greasing

½ cup firmly packed light brown sugar

⅔ cup golden raisins

1½ tablespoons cornstarch, mixed with 2 tablespoons of water

2¼ pounds ready-to-bake puff pastry

all-purpose flour, for dusting

1 egg, beaten with 1 tablespoon water

2 tablespoons raw brown sugar

1 Grease a large baking sheet and set aside. Put the apples, butter, brown sugar, and golden raisins into a large, deep skillet and heat over low heat, stirring, until the butter has melted and the sugar has dissolved. Cover and simmer for 10–15 minutes, until the apples are tender.

2 Stir the cornstarch mixture until it forms a smooth paste and add into the pan. Simmer for another 5 minutes, stirring continuously, until the liquid has thickened. Remove from the heat and let cool.

3 Roll out half the pastry on a lightly floured surface to a thickness of about ⅜ inch. Place the paper template on the dough and use a sharp knife to cut out the triangle shape. Sprinkle the prepared baking sheet with a little cold water and place the pastry triangle on it. Preheat the oven to 425°F.

You will also need...

A triangle paper template, about 13 inches along the two short sides and 16 inches along the long side.

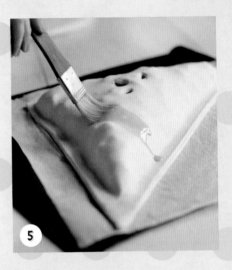

4 Spoon the cold apple filling on top of the pastry, leaving a 1¼-inch border all around. Brush the exposed pastry with cold water.

5 Roll out the remaining pastry to a slightly larger triangle and drape over the filling. Firmly press together the edges of the pastry to seal, trim with a sharp knife, and crimp with your fingertips. Brush the top of the turnover with the beaten egg mixture and sprinkle with the raw brown sugar. Pierce three small holes in the pastry to let the steam escape.

6 Bake the turnover in the preheated oven for 35–45 minutes, until risen and golden brown. Cover loosely with aluminum foil if the pastry starts to brown too much. Serve warm or cold.

Massive Monster Cupcake

Zombie-based baking is trendy right now, so grab yourself a giant piece of the action.

SERVES: 12–14   PREP TIME: 2 hours   COOK TIME: 1 hour 20 mins–1 hour 30 mins

INGREDIENTS

6 ounces semisweet chocolate

3 tablespoons milk

3 cups all-purpose flour,
plus extra for dusting

1¾ teaspoons baking powder

¼ cup unsweetened cocoa powder

3 sticks butter, softened,
plus extra for greasing

1½ cups firmly packed light brown sugar

6 extra-large eggs

TO ASSEMBLE AND DECORATE

1½ pounds white ready-to-use fondant

confectioners' sugar, for dusting

black food coloring

red, yellow, and black writing icing

1 quantity Basic Buttercream (see page 5)

green food coloring paste

1 To prepare the decorations for the cake, line a cutting board with parchment paper. Use a little black food coloring to color about one-fourth of the fondant pale gray. Shape a zombie head, hands, and headstone out of the fondant. Roll two tiny balls from the remaining white fondant for the zombie eyes and mark the eyes and mouth with red and black writing icing. Color a little of the remaining fondant a darker gray and shape into four "rats." Use the yellow tube of writing icing for the rats' eyes. Place all the decorations on the prepared board and let stand in a cool place overnight until set.

2 Preheat the oven to 325°F. Thoroughly grease the cupcake mold with butter, then dust lightly with flour, tipping out any excess. Place the prepared molds on a baking sheet and set aside.

You will
also need...

A giant cupcake mold
with a 5-cup capacity bottom
and a 3½-cup top, and
a fine paintbrush
for decorating.

Hints & tips

Add the green food coloring to the buttercream when beating in the confectioners' sugar and vanilla extract (see page 5 for method) for an even distribution of the color.

3 Put the chocolate and milk into a bowl set over a double boiler or a saucepan of simmering water and heat until the chocolate has melted. Stir until smooth, then let cool for 10 minutes.

4 Sift the flour, baking powder, and cocoa powder into a large mixing bowl and add the remaining cake ingredients. Beat with a handheld electric mixer for 1–2 minutes, until the batter is pale and creamy. Fold in the melted chocolate. Divide the batter between the prepared molds, making a slight dip in the center of each.

5 Bake in the preheated oven for 1 hour 20 minutes, or until risen, golden, and a toothpick inserted into each cake comes out clean. Remove the top cake from the oven, and bake the bottom cake for an additional 10 minutes. Remove the bottom cake from the oven and let both cakes cool in the molds for 10–15 minutes, then carefully turn out onto a cooling rack and let cool completely.

6 To assemble and decorate the cake, prepare the buttercream by mixing in a little green food coloring paste to create a pale green color.

7 Trim the top of each cake to create a level surface (reserving some of the cake scraps). Place the bottom cake upside down on a board and spread a thin layer of buttercream all over the cake. Color any remaining fondant green by kneading in a little food coloring paste. Roll out the fondant on a surface dusted with confectioners' sugar to an 11-inch circle. Drape the fondant over the bottom cake smoothing the sides. Carefully lift the cake and place it upright on a cake board or flat plate. Fold the edges of the fondant over the top of the cake, trimming off any excess.

8 Spread a layer of buttercream over the top of the bottom cake. Position the top cake firmly on the bottom cake. Spread and swirl the remaining buttercream all over the top cake. Crumble the reserved cake scraps and sprinkle them over the buttercream to resemble soil.

9 Use the paintbrush to decorate the headstone with a little black food coloring. Gently push the headstone, zombie head, hands, and cross into the cake and place the rats around them. Pipe a little red writing icing around the hands to resemble blood.

Pancake Peak

A massive mountain of pancakes smothered in maple syrup, perfect for a pancake party.

SERVES: 18   PREP TIME: 40 mins   COOK TIME: 1 hour–1 hours 30 mins

INGREDIENTS

11¼ cups all-purpose flour

⅓ cup plus 2 teaspoons baking powder

½ teaspoon salt

⅓ cup granulated sugar

12 extra-large eggs

about 8 cups milk (see method)

1¼ sticks butter, melted and cooled, plus extra for frying

2½ cups maple syrup and fresh fruit, to serve

YOU WILL ALSO NEED

2 large mixing bowls

9-inch skillet

1 Sift together half the flour, half the baking powder, and half the salt into a large bowl. Stir in half the sugar and make a well in the center. Beat 6 eggs in a small bowl, then pour into the well. Gradually whisk the eggs into the dry mixture with a wire whisk.

2 When some of the flour has been incorporated, start gradually pouring 3¾ cups of the milk into the bowl. Continue whisking, adding more of the milk and drawing in the flour from the sides of the bowl, until a smooth, thick batter forms. Whisk in half the melted butter.

3 Repeat with the remaining batter ingredients to make another large bowl of batter. Cover both bowls of batter and let stand for 30 minutes. Preheat the oven to 275°F. Line two large baking sheets with parchment paper and set aside.

4 Heat a little butter in a skillet until sizzling. Pour a ladleful of batter into the skillet, swirling the skillet to coat the bottom. Cook over medium heat, until bubbles appear on the surface. Use a spatula to flip the pancake and cook for 1 minute, until just cooked. Slide the pancake onto one of the prepared baking sheets and place in the oven to keep warm.

5 Repeat with the remaining batter to make about 18 pancakes in total, stacking the cooked pancakes on top of each other in the warm oven. If the batter becomes too thick, whisk in a little more milk to thin.

6 Pile up the hot pancakes on a large, warm serving platter. Pour some of the maple syrup over the stack, top with fresh fruit, and serve with the remaining maple syrup on the side.

Mega Muffin

Bursting with blueberries, this big breakfast bake is large enough to feed a crowd.

SERVES: 12   PREP TIME: 20 mins   COOK TIME: 1 hour 15 mins – 1 hour 25 mins

INGREDIENTS

3⅔ cups all-purpose flour

5 teaspoons baking powder

1 teaspoon baking soda

1 cup granulated sugar

1½ sticks butter, chilled

2 extra-large eggs

1¼ cups milk

1¼ cups fresh blueberries

1 Preheat the oven to 400°F/. Place the mold on a baking sheet. Ease the parchment paper into the mold, pressing it into the bottom and folding the excess paper into pleats that are smoothed firmly against the sides of the mold. Set aside.

2 Sift together the flour, baking powder, and baking soda into a large bowl. Stir in the sugar. Using a cheese grater, coarsely grate the chilled butter into the bowl. Stir with a fork to coat the butter in the flour mixture. Make a well in the center.

You will also need...

A 5-cup capacity giant cupcake mold (bottom only) and a 13-inch square sheet of parchment paper to make the wrapper.

3 Beat together the eggs and milk and pour into the well. Lightly mix with a fork until just combined. Be careful to avoid overbeating the batter—it should still be lumpy. Gently fold in 1 cup of the blueberries.

4 Spoon the batter into the lined mold. Sprinkle in the remaining blueberries. Bake in the preheated oven for 50 minutes, then reduce the oven temperature to 350°F. Bake for an additional 25–35 minutes, until risen, golden, and a toothpick inserted into the center comes out clean. Let cool in the mold. Once completely cold, remove from the mold and serve with or without the paper liner.

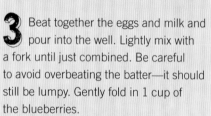

Hints & tips

Great news for lazy bakers— muffin batter needs minimal mixing, and should be left a little lumpy before adding to the mold!

Chunky Chocolate Donut

Even the sprinkles have been enlarged on this gigantic goodie!

SERVES: 12   PREP TIME: 45–50 mins (plus cooling)   COOK TIME: 45–55 mins

INGREDIENTS

⅔ cup unsweetened cocoa powder

⅔ cup boiling water

2½ sticks butter, softened,
plus extra for greasing

1¼ cups firmly packed light brown sugar

5 eggs, beaten

2¼ cups all-purpose flour,
plus extra for dusting

2¼ teaspoons baking powder

4 ounces white ready-to-use fondant

red food coloring

2 tablespoons apricot preserves, warmed

ICING

5 ounces semisweet chocolate

2 tablespoons butter

1 tablespoon light corn syrup

⅔ cup heavy cream

1 Preheat the oven to 325°F. Thoroughly grease the molds, then lightly dust with flour, tipping out any excess. Place the prepared molds on a large baking sheet.

2 Mix together the cocoa powder and boiling water until a smooth paste forms, then set aside. Put the butter and sugar into a large mixing bowl and beat together until pale and creamy. Gradually beat in the eggs, then beat in the cocoa paste. Sift in the flour and baking powder, then gently fold it in.

3 Divide the batter between the prepared molds. Bake in the preheated oven for 45–55 minutes, until the cakes are risen and firm to the touch and a toothpick inserted into the center comes out clean. Let cool in the molds for 10–15 minutes, then carefully turn out onto a wire rack to cool completely.

You will also need...

A silicone donut cake-mold containing two 3-cup molds.

4 To make the sprinkles, divide the ready-to-use fondant into two pieces. Set one aside, and mix the other with a little red food coloring, kneading until the fondant is pink. Roll out the pink and white fondants into two cylindrical lengths, then trim to smaller pieces, each measuring about 1 inch. Round the trimmed edges of the fondant pieces and then set aside in a cool place.

5 To make the icing, break the chocolate into pieces, then put it, the butter, and corn syrup into a double boiler or a large bowl set over a saucepan of simmering water and heat until melted, stirring occasionally. Remove from the heat and stir in the cream to make a thick icing. Let stand for 10–20 minutes, stirring occasionally, until thickened.

6 To assemble, level the tops of each cake with a serrated knife. Place one cake on a serving plate and spread with the preserves. Top with the second cake. Spread a thin layer of the icing all over the cake, then spoon over a second, thicker layer, letting the icing run down the sides of the donut. Decorate with the sprinkles and let stand in a cool place until the icing has set.

Share-Size Sundae

Be the host with the most with this fantastic frozen centerpiece!

SERVES: 12–15   **PREP TIME:** 30 mins (plus freezing)   **COOK TIME:** No cooking

INGREDIENTS

4 quarts good-quality ice cream

2 cups heavy cream

2 bananas

8 ounces strawberries

½ cup chocolate sauce

6 ounces store-bought chocolate brownies, cut into small chunks

½ cup miniature marshmallows

4 ounces mixed candies, such as jelly beans, gum drops, and candy-coated chocolates

⅓ cup raspberry sauce

1–2 tablespoons sprinkles

2 tablespoons chocolate shavings

few maraschino cherries on stems (optional)

1 Remove the ice cream from the freezer and let stand at room temperature for 10–15 minutes to soften a little. Using the ice cream scoop, place scoops of the ice cream on the prepared baking sheets. You should have 40–48 scoops. Place in the freezer on the sheets for 2–3 hours, until solid.

2 When you are ready to assemble the sundae, pour the cream into a bowl and whip until it holds soft peaks. Spoon into a large pastry bag fitted with a large star tip.

3 Peel and slice the bananas and hull and halve the strawberries. Warm the chocolate sauce in the microwave for a few seconds or put it in a double boiler or a bowl set over a saucepan of simmering water for 5–10 minutes.

4 Remove the ice cream from the freezer and pile into the serving bowl together with the fruit, brownies, marshmallows, and nearly all the candies. Drizzle with the raspberry sauce. Pipe rosettes of cream all over the sundae. Sprinkle with the remaining candies and the sprinkles. Top with the chocolate shavings and maraschino cherries, if using, and drizzle with the chocolate sauce. Serve immediately.

1

2

3

You will also need...

An ice cream scoop, three baking sheets lined with baking parchment, and a large serving bowl, at least 12 inches wide and 4 inches deep.

Mammoth Mint Cream

This minty chocolate disk will certainly cause a stir when served as an after-dinner treat.

SERVES: 12–15   PREP TIME: 30 mins (plus setting)   COOK TIME: 10 mins

INGREDIENTS

1 extra-large egg white

few drops of lemon juice

1–2 teaspoons peppermint extract

about 3⅔ cups confectioners' sugar (see method), plus extra for dusting

8 ounces semisweet chocolate, broken into pieces

1 Line a board with a sheet of parchment paper. Put the egg white, lemon juice, and peppermint extract into a large bowl and whisk with a fork until frothy.

2 Gradually beat in the confectioners' sugar until a stiff paste forms. Lightly knead until smooth, adding more confectioners' sugar if the paste is too sticky.

3 Shape into a flat patty on a surface dusted with confectioners' sugar, then roll out to an 8-inch circle. Place on the prepared board. Loosely cover with plastic wrap and let stand in a cool, dry place overnight, turning once, until firm and dry.

Pretty pastels

For a pretty pastel finish, cover the outside of the chocolate shell with a thin layer of candy melts (as used on page 18) to create a colorful coating.

4 Place the chocolate in a double boiler or a heatproof bowl set over a saucepan of barely simmering water, being careful that the bottom of the bowl doesn't come in contact with the water, and heat until melted. Remove from the heat and stir until smooth. Let cool for 10 minutes.

5 Spread a thin layer of the melted chocolate over the top and sides of the peppermint cream with a small spatula. Chill in the refrigerator for 20 minutes, until just set. Spread the remaining melted chocolate over the top of the peppermint cream and let stand in a cool place for 1–2 hours, until set.

6 Carefully remove the peppermint cream from the parchment paper and place on a serving plate. It will keep for up to two weeks, covered, in a cool dry place.

Orange options

If mint isn't your thing and you prefer an orangey-zing to your chocolate, swap the peppermint extract for orange extract, to taste.

Chock-a-Block Cookie Sandwich

Two chunky chocolate cookies stuck together with a great big dollop of sweet buttercream filling.

SERVES: 12   PREP TIME: 40 mins (plus chilling)   COOK TIME: 40–50 mins

INGREDIENTS

3¾ cups all-purpose flour

1 cup unsweetened cocoa powder

1 teaspoon baking powder

½ teaspoon salt

4 sticks butter, softened,
plus extra for greasing

1¾ cups granulated sugar

2 extra-large egg yolks, lightly beaten

1 teaspoon vanilla extract

BUTTERCREAM FILLING

1½ sticks butter, softened

2 teaspoons vanilla extract

red food coloring

2⅓ cups confectioners' sugar

1 Grease and line the bottom of both tart pans and set aside. Sift together the flour, cocoa, and baking powder into a large bowl and add the salt. Set aside.

2 Put the butter and sugar into a large bowl and beat with a handheld electric mixer until fluffy. Add the egg yolks and vanilla extract and beat until smooth. Add half the flour mixture and continue beating until just incorporated. Add the remaining flour and stir with a wooden spoon until the mixture starts to clump together. Gather the mixture into a ball with your hands and gently knead until smooth (the dough will be soft and sticky at this stage).

You will also need ...

Two 8-inch round, loose-bottom fluted tart pans.

2

3

Hints & tips

Invest a little extra time into preparing the tart pans before adding the cookie dough— it's a dense, gooey mixture that's prone to sticking.

3 Divide the dough into two pieces and press into the prepared pans, using your fingers or a small spatula to smooth and flatten the dough. Chill in the refrigerator for 40 minutes. Meanwhile, preheat the oven to 350°F.

4 Place the pans onto two baking sheets and bake the cookies in the preheated oven for 40–50 minutes, or until the tops look set and feel just firm to the touch. Let cool in the pans for 15 minutes, then carefully turn out onto a wire rack to cool completely.

5 To make the filling, put the butter, vanilla extract, and 1 teaspoon of food coloring into a large bowl and beat with a handheld electric mixer until pale and creamy. Gradually beat in the confectioners' sugar to make a smooth buttercream. Spread one cookie with the buttercream and place in the refrigerator for 30 minutes, until firm. Top with the second cookie, pressing down gently.

Tremendous Truffles

These tennis ball-size chocolate truffles are definitely much too big for just one chocolate lover.

SERVES: 4–6 each   **PREP TIME:** 40 mins (plus chilling)   **COOK TIME:** 10 mins

INGREDIENTS

14 ounces semisweet chocolate, broken into pieces

1 stick unsalted butter

1¼ cups heavy cream

2 tablespoons brandy (optional)

1 tablespoon confectioners' sugar

1 tablespoon unsweetened cocoa powder

YOU WILL ALSO NEED

4 muffin cups

1 Place the chocolate and butter in a double boiler or a large, heatproof bowl set over a saucepan of barely simmering water and heat until both have melted, stirring occasionally. Remove the bowl from the heat and stir until smooth.

2 Gradually stir in the cream and brandy, if using. Let cool for 10 minutes, then beat the mixture with a handheld electric mixer for 3–4 minutes, until thickened. Cover and chill in the refrigerator for 3–4 hours, until the mixture is firm.

3 Sprinkle the sugar on a plate and sprinkle the cocoa powder on a separate plate. Divide the chocolate mixture into four pieces and, with cold hands, quickly roll each piece into a ball. Roll two truffles in the sugar and the remaining two in the cocoa powder.

4 Place the truffles in muffin cups and chill in the refrigerator (they will keep for up to one week). Let stand at room temperature for about an hour before serving to let them soften slightly.

Sprinkles

Roll the chocolate truffle balls into colorful sprinkles, instead of cocoa powder or confectioners' sugar, to create vibrant chocolates.

Super Sweet & Salted Pretzels

Soft and doughy, with a light crisp shell, these are the ultimate snack.

SERVES: 6–8 each   PREP TIME: 40 mins (plus rising and freezing)   COOK TIME: 15–20 mins

INGREDIENTS

3⅔ cups white bread flour

1 teaspoon salt

1½ teaspoons active dry yeast

1 cup lukewarm water

3 tablespoons butter, melted, plus extra for greasing

1 egg yolk, beaten with 1 tablespoon water

1 teaspoon coarse sea salt

8 ounces semisweet chocolate, broken into pieces

YOU WILL ALSO NEED

large, deep skillet or wok

2 tablespoons baking soda

1 Grease and line two baking sheets and set aside. Put the flour, salt, and yeast into a large bowl, make a well in the center and stir in the water and butter. Mix to a soft dough, then turn out onto a lightly floured surface and knead for 6–8 minutes, until smooth, adding a little more flour if the dough is sticky.

2 Divide the dough into two pieces and roll out each piece to a long thin strip about 4 feet long. Shape each strip into a large pretzel and place on one of the prepared baking sheets. Let stand, uncovered, in a warm place for 45–55 minutes, until puffy. Transfer the pretzels on the baking sheets to the freezer for 1 hour.

Hints & tips

Poaching in alkaline water (created by the baking soda) is essential for achieving a shiny, crisp crust and doughy, soft middle.

2

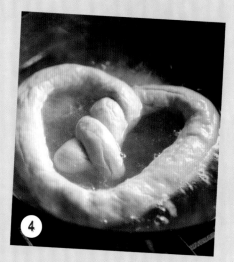

4

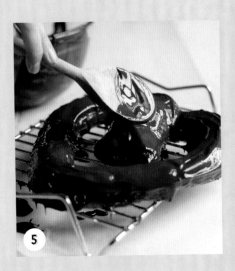

5

3 Fill a large, deep skillet or wok with water and add the baking soda. Bring to a boil. Preheat the oven to 425°F.

4 Place one semifrozen pretzel in the boiling water and cook for 2 minutes. Meanwhile, remove and discard the parchment paper from the baking sheet and grease with butter. Carefully lift out the pretzel (you'll need a couple of spatulas to do this) and place on the greased baking sheet. Brush the pretzel all over with the egg yolk mixture and sprinkle with sea salt. Bake in the preheated oven for 15–20 minutes, until deep golden brown. Transfer to a wire rack to cool. Boil and bake the second pretzel in the same way but don't sprinkle with salt.

5 To make the chocolate coating, place the chocolate in a double boiler or a heatproof bowl set over a saucepan of gently simmering water, being careful that the bottom of the bowl doesn't touch the water, and heat until melted. Let cool for 15 minutes, then transfer to a wire rack and spoon three-quarters of the chocolate over to cover the pretzel completely. Let stand in a cool place until the chocolate has set. Then spread with the remaining chocolate and let cool completely.

Index

apples 45
Awesome Apple Turnover
   44–47
bananas 62
beans, chocolate 8, 21
beans, dried 17
blueberries 55
Bountiful Cinnamon Roll
   38–41
brandy 72
bun 38–41
buttercream 5, 8, 17, 49
candies, mixed 62
cherries
   candied 8
   maraschino 62
Choc-a-Block Cookie
   Sandwich 68–71
chocolate
   beans 8, 21
   milk 11, 35
   sauce 62
   semisweet 35, 49, 59, 65,
   72, 75
   shavings 62
   chocolate brownies 62
Chunky Chocolate Donut
   58–61

cinnamon 39
cocoa powder 42, 49, 59,
   69, 72
Colossal Cake Pops 16–19
confectioners' sugar 8, 17,
   21, 32, 35, 39, 49, 69, 72
cookies
   chocolate 10–13, 20–23,
   68–71
   heart-shape 32–33
   truffles 72–73
cooking times 5
cupcakes 5, 8–9, 48–51
donuts 5, 58–61
Double-Dunk Choc-Chunk
   Cookie 10–13
eggs 8, 21, 25, 29, 32, 39,
   42,
   45, 49, 52, 55, 59, 65, 69,
   75
Foot-High Festive Cookie
   20–23
fruit 52
   bananas 62
   blueberries 55
   maraschino cherries 62
   raspberries 29
   strawberries 62

giant food, general tips 4–5
Giant Frosted Cupcake 8–9
gingerbread 24–27
Ginormous Gingerbread Man
   24–27
golden raisins 45
Humongous Heart Cookie
   32–33
ice cream 62, 64–67
macaron 28–31
Mammoth Mint Cream 64–67
marshmallows 2, 62
Massive Monster Cupcake
   48–49
Mega Muffin 54–57
Mighty Macaron 28–31
mint, ice cream 64–67
muffins 5, 54–57
nuts
   almonds 29
   macadamia 11
   pecans 11, 39
pancake 52–53
Pancake Peak 52–53
Party-Size Popcorn Ball
   14–15
pastry, puff 45
peanut butter 35

pie wieghts 17
Plentiful Peanut Butter Cup
   34–37
popcorn 14–15
popping corn 14
pound cake 17
preserves
   apricot 8, 59
   raspberry 29
pretzels 74–77
raspberry 29
   sauce 62
Share-Size Sundae 62
sponge 8–9, 42–43
strawberries 62
Super Sweet & Salted Pretzels
   74–77
syrup 11, 14, 25, 52, 59
Tremendous Truffles 72–73
Whopping Whoopie Pie
   42–43

NOTES FOR THE READER

This book uses standard kitchen measuring spoons and cups. All spoon and cup measurements are level unless otherwise indicated. Unless otherwise stated, milk is assumed to be whole, butter is assumed to be salted, eggs are large, individual vegetables are medium, and pepper is freshly ground black pepper.

Garnishes and serving suggestions are all optional and not necessarily included in the recipe ingredients or method.

The times given are only an approximate guide. Preparation times differ according to the techniques used by different people and the cooking times may also vary from those given. Optional ingredients, variations, or serving suggestions have not been included in the calculations.

Recipes using raw or very lightly cooked eggs should be avoided by infants, the elderly, pregnant women, and people with weakened immune systems. Pregnant and breast-feeding women are advised to avoid eating peanuts and peanut products. People with nut allergies should be aware that some of the prepared ingredients used in the recipes in this book may contain nuts. Always check the packaging before use.

Vegetarians should be aware that some of the prepared ingredients used in the recipes in this book may contain animal products. Always check the package before use.

First published in 2013
LOVE FOOD is an imprint of Parragon Books Ltd

Parragon
Chartist House
15–17 Trim Street
Bath, BA1 1HA, UK

www.parragon.com/lovefood

ISBN: 978-1-4723-1104-7

Printed in China

Recipe photography by Mike Cooper
Home economy by Sumi Glass
Incidental photography by Henry Sparrow
Recipes and introduction by Angela Drake
Design by Geoff Borin